Retrieving the lives of two female disciples of Sri Ramakrishna in 19th century Bengal: Lakshmi Devi, a girl widow and Yogin-Ma, a dissolute *babu's* wife.
The Need for Archival Research.

TAPATI BHARADWAJ

DEDICATION

To our foremothers.

CONTENTS

Acknowledgments

ACKNOWLEDGMENTS

It took me a while to really understand what it took for women in the long nineteenth century in Bengal, India, who were relegated to the private realm, to conform to strict gender roles. I was helped by the fact that I live in the present in India, in spaces which are filled with stay at home mothers who cook and look after children and manage the socio-emotional economy of the household. The demands of motherhood in India are so high that these women cannot think of a world outside the home. To what extent have they internalized what has been taught to them by their parents/society? I never did find any stay at home father. But I still have lots of time to find out all my answers to my queries.

1 INTRODUCTION

The lives of women who were living in nineteenth century Bengal, India is a subject that much can be written about. Feminist historians have worked towards recuperating their voices but we still hear narratives that reflect only some of the lives of women; the most important element in this act of writing would be tracing and locating primary and secondary sources which will allow us to even achieve some kind of proximity with them. Of more relevance is the fact that often we are also unable to determine what interpretative parameters to use when reading these sources. We cannot homogenize the lives of all women who were living in nineteenth century Bengal, and we have to understand them, keeping in mind that class and caste were important determining factors in their lives.

In this book, I look at the lives of two female disciples of Sri Ramakrishna, the mystic saint who lived in the nineteenth century, at Dakshineshwar, near Calcutta. The lives of these two women is reasonably documented, and yet we know very little about them in feminist histories, unless one happens to read the publications of the Ramakrishna Mission.[1] Of course, the question that is inevitable is this: why do we need to know about them at all as they would have led conventional lives within the domain of married domesticity, raising children and involved in domestic labor, as was the norm for

---

[1] All incidents from the lives of Lakshmi Devi and Yogin-Ma are from Swami Chetananda's *They Lived With God: Life Stories of Some Devotees of Sri Ramakrishna* (Calcutta: Advaita Ashram, 1991).

1

all women in nineteenth century Bengal. Of tantamount importance is the fact that these two female disciples, who were born in quite conservative families, were able to occupy a space in the semi-public realm of the religious-spiritual, through their involvement with Sri Ramakrishna. They were at par with the male devotees and disciples of Sri Ramakrishna, and that is saying a lot. Sri Ramakrishna ensured that there was parity between his male and his female disciples.

What we know about Sri Ramakrishna is based on interpretations that have been written about him; more often than not, they are hagiographical in nature and not surprisingly so. This hagiographical element has monopolized that nature of the dialogue that exists on Sri Ramakrishna, oftentimes eliding the fact that the social commentaries that he made were very specific to that time period and cannot be construed in an ahistorical manner. But what is quite interesting is that Sri Ramakrishna was actually quite socially transgressive for his time period, considering the fact that he was an illiterate Brahmin-priest from rural Bengal, and we never really get to hear this about him. He was supposed to maintain the status quo which was represented and disseminated by patriarchal, Hindu institutions. His all-embracing perspective allowed him to reach out to all, disregarding colonizer and colonized.

Even though, Sri Ramakrishna was born in rural Bengal, at a time period when the Britishers were ruling the country, and Indians were the subjects, he never actually distinguished people on the basis of their nationality. An incident from his life was narrated by Lakshmi Devi, his niece and one of his female disciples, and thereby, we learn about his capacity to love everyone:

One day I went with [Holy] Mother to carry Thakur his food. Rakhal and others who were with him, at once left the room, leaving us alone. Thakur was lying on his bed in *Samadhi*, but he looked so devoid of life that Mother, having long been anxious for his health, began to weep thinking he had left the body. Then she remembered that he had once said to her that if she ever found him in this state she was just to touch his feet and that would bring him back; so she began to rub his feet. Rakhal and the others hearing the weeping had also hurried back into the room and they too began to rub him vigorously.

This brought him back to consciousness, and opening his eyes he asked with surprise what was the matter. Then realising his fear, he smiled and said, "I was in the land of the white people. Their skin is white and their hearts are white and they are simple and sincere. It is a very beautiful country. I think I shall go there."[2]

Why did Sri Ramakrishna articulate such appreciation about the western world? The accepted behaviour would have been for him to show anger and animosity about the West, and yet he did not. He was able to understand the fact that the West did represent a civilizational change from India; he was able to undo the dichotomy of colonized/Indian and colonizer/ West and reach out to a greater understanding of what the West stood for.

His method of subverting social norms was quite unusual; once, Sri Ramakrishna persuaded Lakshmi Devi, his widowed niece and disciple, to eat a piece of fish that had been served to the Goddess Kali as *prasad*. Even though she hesitated, Sri Ramakrishna was able to convince her that it was alright for her to eat it. For an upper caste widow to eat fish was an act of social transgression, and this was couched by the fact that it was an offering to God. What was more transgressive was the fact that it had been validated by Sri Ramakrishna himself, a priest and a religious man – the very person who should have been the guardian against such socially transgressive behaviour.

---

[2] Quoted in Ibid., p. 64; from Sister Devamata's *Days in an Indian Monastery* (California: Ananda Ashrama, 1927), pp. 283-84.

In this book, I argue that Sri Ramakrishna's acts of gender inclusion in an essentially male domain of Hindu religion in the nineteenth century is a historical fact that has been elided by feminist scholars; more surprisingly, all hagiographical narratives on Sri Ramakrishna, published by the Ramakrishna Mission, are also silent about this. I would argue that this ethical act of inclusion can be seen as akin to the 73rd Amendment Act which was passed by the Government of India in 1993 and was meant to empower the rural subaltern of India. This Indian bill was implemented by the state and provided reservation for women in the local governing bodies (the *Panchayati* system of local self rule where each village unit elected it's members and heads to supervise the political activities). What Sri Ramakrishna was suggesting is that there should be parity in the realm of religion, and he ensured that it happened; whether subsequently, the Ramakrishna Mission was able to keep up to this proposal is another issue altogether. It is one thing to theorize and another to put the theory into praxis; Sri Ramakrishna did put his feminist position into practice. It is not an exaggeration to draw parallels between the role of Hindu religion in our everyday lives and the role played by the Indian state in determining how we live as citizens; they address and safeguard different aspects of our being. By looking at the manner in which Sri Ramakrishna was able to guide his two female disciples into an essentially male domain of religion in the nineteenth century, we learn about his capacity for enormous empathy which allowed him ethical solidarity with these women. A hundred years later or so, the state performed a similar function when it empowered women to participate in the Panchayat system.

I also argue that due to a lack of primary and secondary resources on the lives of women in the nineteenth century, archival research needs to be done. Doing so will allow for the emergence of a new discipline in feminist history on the lives of women in nineteenth century Bengal.

In the concluding chapters, I examine the lives of Lakshmi Devi (1864-1926), Sri Ramakrishna's niece, and Yogin-Ma (1851-1924), and both were disciples of the Master. Lakshmi Devi was a child widow, and Yogin-Ma was the daughter of Prasanna Mitra, a doctor of the Calcutta Medical College and was quite involved with the Young Bengals; Yogin-Ma left his dissolute husband and lived at her maternal home most of her adult life.

Recuperating the lives of women who lived in the inner realms of the domestic in nineteenth century Bengal is indeed an uphill task. As I put the pieces of their lives together, I often wondered whether they were happy. I wondered what their worlds comprised of and whether they ever desired to enter the public worlds, as they saw their fathers and brothers and husbands work in very public domains. Were they unhappy because their gender predetermined their labour and their position in society? This book is just the beginning of a dialogue that hopefully will continue and grow.

2 TOWARDS EQUALITY

It is important to address ways of understanding the
conditions or circumstances under which it is possible for women to
achieve parity within Indian society. I will argue that as we look at the
lives of the women who were involved in the life of Sri Ramakrishna
in the nineteenth century, we are able to gauge how he ensured that
they did achieve spiritual parity; this means that as devotees, who
desired spiritual guidance, they were guided in the same manner as
were their male counterparts. In the absence of equality in the public
realm, which would take place subsequently after Independence, Sri
Ramakrishna negotiated against dominant social norms and created
spaces which allowed for women to be at par with men in the realm
of the religious. This undoubtedly is not quantifiable – what do we
mean when we say that women were equals in this realm? This
concept can come across as a paradox as these female disciples
conformed to social expectations in all respects and were often quite
invisible in the public sphere.

It is only when we look at the lives of Lakshmi Devi and Yogin-
Ma, which we will in the following chapters, we realize what it meant
to be a woman in nineteenth century Bengal, India. Obviously, these
are isolated incidents, and forgotten by mainstream Indian society and
feminist history tends to elide the fact that Sri Ramakrishna gave
parity to women in the realm of the spiritual at a time period in Indian
history when women were really not at parity in other public spheres.
The question is: why do we erase this fact from our public

consciousness? By recuperating these narratives and rewriting them, we retrieve forgotten histories and in the process, a more nuanced and multilayered notion of history emerges.

The enormity of Sri Ramakrishna's actions can be gauged if we draw an analogy with him and the workings of the Indian state and the steps it has taken to compel participation of women in the public realm. This chapter looks at how the state empowered women in the realm of the public through compulsory participation at the Panchayat system of self-governance.

The Indian Constitution in 1947 declared equality as a fundamental right. It also guaranteed equal protection under the law, provided equal opportunities in public employment, and prohibited discrimination in public places. Equality was constructed as being accessible to all and did not take into account that each individual, being located within different social realities, were not similarly positioned to enact this concept. This rhetoric, which existed at the discursive level, did not affect women materially. The Indian Government's commitment to equality was seriously challenged and critiqued in 1974 when "Towards Equality,"[3] a report on the status of women was published. In 1971, the Ministry of Education and Social Welfare had appointed a committee "to examine the constitutional, legal and administrative provisions that have a bearing on the social status of women, their education and employment" and to assess the impact of these provisions.[4] The research and it's publication were also, partly, in response to a United Nations request to all countries to prepare reports on the status of women for International

---

[3] *A Report on Towards Equality* by The Committee on the Status of Women in India; India. Ministry of Education and Social Welfare (New Delhi: Dept of Social Welfare, Ministry of Education and Social Welfare, 1974).

[4] Ibid, p. 114.

Women's Year, scheduled for 1975. The report concluded by stating that the status of women had not improved since Independence, and is worth quoting at length:

> Social structures, cultural norms, and value systems influence social expectations regarding the behavior of both men and women, and determine a woman's role and her position in society to a great extent. The most important of these institutions are the systems of descent, family and kinship, marriage, and religious traditions. ... The normative standards do not change at the same pace as changes in other forms of social organization brought about by such factors as technological and educational advances, urbanization, increasing populations. .... This gap explains the frequent failure of law and educational policy to produce the desired effect on social attitudes.[5]

In this report to the government of India, the native informants, i.e. the members of the committee, concluded by recommending (amongst other things) "establishment of women's *panchayats* at the village level with autonomy and resources of their own for the management and administration of welfare and development programs."[6]

The 73rd Amendment Act which was passed by the Government of India in 1993 was meant to empower the rural subaltern of India. Here, I have elaborated on the manner in which this Indian bill was implemented by the state machinery (as a result of demands made by feminist non-governmental organizations and female parliamentary members), and how it provided reservation for women in the local

---

[5] Ibid., pp. 114-115.

[6] Ibid., pp. 114-115.

governing bodies (the *Panchayati* system of local self rule where each village unit elected it's members and heads to supervise the political activities). This decision to empower the rural women of India was not a result of their own awareness of gender inequalities in the political sphere and consequently their demand for changes. The bill thus makes the whole notion of experiential knowledge suspect; it was hoped that "reservation of seats in the *Panchayati Raj* Institutions (local self government units) and municipal bodies (would) provide them (the subalterns') with an opportunity to ventilate their grievances and to take active part in the formal political arena which deals with social and economic problems."[7] By facilitating the subalterns' entry into this public space, the Bill would subsequently enable them to conceptualize themselves differently -- as having the agency to desire or negate this empowerment.

Subtle ideological changes are possible if made through state and government intervention; my position here does not sanction or legitimate government entry into private lives, but rather simply states that sometimes, legal legislation has the power to provide necessary spaces to marginal groups -- spaces which have hitherto, been denied to them. The state can indeed play an effective and benevolent role, one which operates on unstated assumptions of ethics. The apparent absence of reasons as to why a non-subaltern would be involved at all haunts both the native and first world scholars, which can be explained away by espousing an ethical stance. If the feminist agenda aims at ensuring socially just systems, those in powerful positions have not only to be aware of their involvement in perpetuating this system but subsequently, through constant interrogation, transmute their involvement into a benevolent one.

This notion should be considered in conjunction with the fact that there exists multiple concepts and contexts of consciousness.

---

[7] Shweta Mishra, "Women and 73rd Amendment Act: A Critical Appraisal" in *Social Action* No. 47 (Jan-Mar.,1997). pp.16-30; p. 16.

The 73rd Amendment Act in India that had been introduced and had compelled the subaltern women to participate in the political structure was not a result of their awareness that they could subvert the gender hierarchies which were present. The lack/presence of critical consciousness might sometimes not result in self-beneficial knowledge production.

Theorizing the presence of multiple levels of consciousness implies that the experiential narratives of some groups would prove to be insufficient for knowledge production. The subaltern woman's lack of desire to participate in the political structure and to subvert the existing gender dynamics might call for the cultivation of an 'intellectual consciousness' (and not a subaltern one), but nonetheless the level at which knowledge production occurs for the subaltern is valuable. The Constitution Bill which provided the possibility of political participation for the subaltern women, operated on the assumption that there existed a subaltern consciousness. This legal intervention conceptualized the subaltern woman as not necessarily displaying overt signs of self-awareness or wanting an entry into the public sphere; this enabled 'native intellectuals' i.e. 'outsiders' to formulate the Bill. Because the subaltern was discursively constructed within these paradigms, the formation of the Bill was affected accordingly and compelled the women to participate.

Women in diverse locations would conceptualize themselves differently -- which implies that it is not possible to expect all Indian women to exhibit similar kinds of behavioral patterns. The dialectics which exists within an individual is succinctly elaborated by Linda Alcoff[8] when she writes that a woman is not a passive recipient constructed by her surroundings but that she "is part of the historicized, fluid movement, and she actively contributes to the

---

[8] Linda Alcoff, "Cultural Feminism versus Post-structucturalism. The identity crisis in Feminist Theory." In *The Second Wave: A Reader in Feminist Theory*, ed. Linda Nicholson (New York: Routledge, 1997), pp. 330-355.

context within which her position can be delineated."[9] Alcoff also states that a woman becomes a feminist, not after she learns new facts about the world (where she is positioned in an oppressive situation) but because she comes to "view those facts from a different position, from [her] own position as [a] subject."[10] As she is a social construct, it is important that we refer to her specific social location and theorize how her environment affects her self-conceptualization. The social and economic roles of women in an Indian peasant society are influenced to a certain extent by traditional customs and by the processes of education and socialization.[9] The manner in which men and women participate in social interaction is determined by their adherence to gender specific roles. It is also important that we do not homogenize rural women; class and caste are important factors determining the location of women.

Taking into consideration the usual gender patterns, it would have been unusual for the subaltern woman to desire and subsequently gain entry into the public sphere of politics. But it can also be argued that despite the subaltern's internalization of gender hierarchies, her complicity within the existing status quo does not inevitably follow. While the subaltern might not be complicit, she still might not necessarily not be in a position to conceptualize the possibility of subverting gender roles by desiring entry into the political structure. Forceful intervention in the subalterns' lives — through the Constitution Bill -- meant that an attempt was being made to subvert the normal social pattern. A change in their behavioral pattern, through the entry of women in the public sphere affected the way they conceptualized each other. The necessity of this kind of legal intervention is made evident when one compares it with other unobtrusive social, political and economic changes which had been visualized by the Government of India.

---

[9] Ibid., pp. 348-349.
[10] Ibid., pp. 348-349.

CONCLUSION.

By drawing an analogy between the Indian state's benevolence and Sri Ramakrishna's involvement in the lives of his female disciples, we are able to understand the extent to which he was ethically committed to ensuring parity at the realm of the spiritual. He understood that women were located in geo-social, cultural spaces and realities which affected their capacity to engage with the public world of mainstream religion. He subverted gender norms of what it meant to be a married, upper class/ caste woman in nineteenth century Bengal and instead, engaged with them to allow them entry in what was a mostly male domain of mainstream Hindu religion.

3 THE NEED FOR ARCHIVAL RESEARCH

In order to create a feminist genealogy in India, we need to be able to incorporate a diverse range of voices of women. I would argue that as there is some documented source on the lives of women who were directly connected to Sri Ramakrishna, we should also embrace these narratives when establishing a tradition of the lives of women who were living in the nineteenth century in India. By locating all sources on their lives, which would undoubtedly be in the archives maintained by the Ramakrishna Mission, we can arrive at a more comprehensive picture of how they lived. More importantly, we should not forget that through these archives, feminist scholars can have access to primary and secondary material which will reveal how women engaged with a dominantly male domain of religion and spirituality in the nineteenth century. Archival research is therefore needed, which will throw more light on the lives of women who were living in the nineteenth century in Bengal. Such kinds of research will also allow for a new discipline to emerge within feminist studies in India. Looking from a larger, cross disciplinary perspective makes one conclude that archival research has unearthed a lot of unexplored territories and established new disciplines.

For example, book history in India relies on archival research and more needs to be done. A lot of the work that is done on early book history in American studies is based on little used and little read archival material. Book history, of the antebellum period, within

American studies often uses minor texts. Matthew Brown's "The Thick Style: Steady Sellers, Textual Aesthetics, and Early Modern Devotional Reading"[11] in the 2006 January edition of the *PMLA* makes use as primary texts devotional writings that were printed in the early seventeenth century in America. These devotional works comprised of "manuals of piety, guides to conversion, sermon series, and psalm books" alongside scriptures which formed the popular literature of early New England and were written by moderate to radical Reformers and Non conformists.[12] Brown argues that these works are little known texts, but can be construed as defining a "literary culture" of the seventeenth century, helping to substantiate the "scroll-to-codex" analogy."[13] In a similar manner, in *The Letters of the Republic*, Michael Warner argues that a transformation of power took place in eighteenth century America as a result of "an increased volume of print" and also because of how printed texts were construed by the reading public; he uses the examples of legal texts, constitutional tracts, writings of Benjamin Franklin, magazines and newspapers of eighteenth century America.[14] The development of the discipline of early book history in American studies was dependent on being able to retrieve and access archived texts.

The discipline of black feminist literary criticism is a recent creation and Barbara Christian's works have been seminal in establishing a literary genealogy of black women writers who were erased from the literary imagination; *Black Women Novelists: The*

---

[11] Matthew P. Brown, "The Thick Style: Steady Sellers, Textual Aesthetics, and Early Modern Devotional Reading." *PMLA*, Vol. 121(1): 67-86.

[12] Ibid.,p. 68.

[13] Ibid., p. 69.

[14] Michael Warner, *Letters of the Republic* (Harvarad, Harvard University Press, 1990).

Development of a Tradition[15] looks at the writings of Zora Neale Hurston and Nella Larsen. On a similar note, her work, *Black Feminist Criticism: Perspectives on black women writers*[16] draws attention to the manner in which she was involved in retrieving a forgotten literary tradition of black women writers. The need to retrieve a lost African American literary tradition is elaborated in another essay[17] where she describes how in the August 1974 edition of *Black World*, the most widely read publication on African American literature, culture and politics of that time, a picture of a then little known writer, Zora Neale Hurston, was used as a picture cover. It implied a "literary foremother who had been neglected by Afro-Americanists of the past but who was finally being recognized by her daughters and reinstated as a major figure in the African American literary tradition."[18] Christian writes that it was "virtually impossible to locate either the works of many 19th century writers or those of contemporary writers;"[19] moreover, there was a dearth of secondary material on these writers in the 1970s. Thus, not only was a new discipline formed, through retrieving forgotten writers but there was a focus on the need to generate scholarship on how to interpret these texts.

Within the Indian context, there are many writers whom we have forgotten, and who were writing in the late eighteenth and early

---

[15] Barbara Christian, *Black Women Novelists: The Development of a Tradition* (Westport, Connecticut: Greenwood Press, 1980).

[16] Barbara Christian, *Black Feminist Criticism: Perspectives on black women writers* (Teachers College Press, 1985).

[17] Barbara Christian, "But What Do We Think We've Being Doing Anyway: The State of Black Feminist Criticism(s) or My Version of a Little Bit of History" in *New Black Feminist Criticism 1985-2000, Barbara Christian*, eds. Gloria Bowles, M. Giulia Febi and Arlene R. Keizer (Urbana: University of Illinois Press, 2007), pp.5-19.

[18] Ibid., p. 5.

[19] Ibid., p. 9.

nineteenth centuries and their works also comprise the first printed texts. The first literary works in India in English were by Englishmen for their personal consumption, and was part of the imperial hegemonic sub public realm of print. That such literary works were locally printed meant the emergence and establishment of a group of editors and literary journals that was conversant with the literary tradition. Eventually, these printed works would allow for and pave the way for natives who would also write in English. Archival research will allow us to figure out the books that were written in the last two decades of the eighteenth century, and a few that we can consider are: *The bevy of Calcutta beauties. A collection of poems,*[20] *The poems of Anna Maria,*[21] *The happy prescription; or, the lady relieved from her lovers: a comedy in rhyme,*[22] *The two connoisseurs; a comedy, in rhyme,*[23] *East India Company. Treaties. Etc,*[24] *Kalidasa. The seasons: A descriptive poem,* by Calidas, in the original Sanskrit,[25]. *A collection of poems, written in the East Indies. With miscellaneous remarks in real life,*[26] *A poem, on the capture of Seringapatnam, by a Bengal officer.*[27] In the early nineteenth century, many literary magazines were also printed in Calcutta and notwithstanding the fact that the emergence of print culture was but twenty years old, a sophisticated realm of literature evolved. Retrieving these archived texts will allow us to conceptualize new methodologies and areas of

---

[20] Published in Calcutta; printed by Daniel Stuart, 1785.

[21] Published in Calcutta; from the press of Thomson and Ferris, 1793.

[22] Written for a private theatre, by William Hayley, Esq. – Calcutta: printed in the year, 1785.

[23] Written for the private theatre, by William Hayley, Esq. – Calcutta; printed in the year, 1785.

[24] Published in Calcutta: printed at the Honourable Company's Press, 1788.

[25] Published in Calcutta; printed at the Honourable Company's Press, 1792.

[26] By John Horsford, Calcutta; printed by Joseph Cooper, Telegraph Press, 1797.

[27] Published in Calcutta; printed at the Telegraph office, 1799.

study in early print culture in colonial Calcutta.

CONCLUSION.

The nineteenth century took place not so long ago and we know little about the lives of our foremothers. The hurdle, though, is in locating primary or secondary texts which allow us to write about their lives; what is noteworthy is the fact that Sri Ramakrishna's life has been carefully documented which implies that there is a lot of documented material which would describe the lives of women who were directly or indirectly associated with him. Accessing these texts would open up a new discipline on the lives of women in nineteenth century feminist history.

What we know about the lives of women who were living in the nineteenth century in India is limited and often than not, viewed with the assumption that patriarchy and Hinduism both kept women oppressed, which of course is a fact. I would argue that we can work towards a more nuanced perspective of the nineteenth century when we broaden our interpretative parameters on how to understand the lives of women who were not in the public realm. When we closely examine the lives of two women, Lakshmi Devi and Yogin Ma, who were disciples of Sri Ramakrishna, we are compelled to conclude they had agency in this realm of the religious-spiritual that was at par with his male disciples.

4 LAKSHMI DEVI (1864-1926)

There is little documented evidence how life was for upper caste women in rural Bengal in the nineteenth century and we get an inking about their lives when we read about Lakshmi Devi(1864-1926), who was Sri Ramakrishna's niece.[28] We cannot elide the fact that her proximity to Sri Ramakrishna meant that her life would be documented by his devotees and disciples. Otherwise, the lives of such women would have been forgotten, and categorised under the broad umbrella of oppressed native women of nineteenth century India. When we closely look at certain events in Lakshmi Devi's life, we are compelled to arrive at interpretative parameters that are more nuanced than the dominant norm of oppressed native women and cannot be contained within it. We need to pry open the larger socio-religious norms under which she lived, and trace her life's trajectory, which will allow us to arrive at ways to understand the choices she made or was not allowed to make. I would argue that religion, and Sri Ramakrishna's presence in her life, gave her social parity in a semi-public realm of religion and this was denied to most women in India in the nineteenth century.

Sri Ramakrishna considered Lakshmi Devi to be a reincarnation of the goddess *Shitala*, one of the family deities of Khudiram, Sri Ramakrishna's father; the other two were Raghurvir (Rama) and Rameshwar Shiva. At Dakshineshwar, Sri Ramakrishna would receive

---

[28] For more, see Swami Chetananda's *They Lived with God: Life Stories of some devotees of Sri Ramakrishna* (Calcutta: Advaita Ashram, 1999). pp. 57-70.

sweets and other delicacies from his devotees; he was sad that that he could not also serve these to his family deity, *Shitala*, at Kamarpukur. Subsequently, he had a dream where he understood that serving Lakshmi, his niece, would be the equivalent of feeding *Shitala* at Kamarpukur. He undid the notion of conceptualising God in the abstract and instead, humanized the act of worship; if he considered Lakshmi as an incarnation of a goddess, then he translated this belief into practise by ensuring that she had greater agency than most rural women in her position. As we look at Laskhmi Devi's life, we realise that she did not participate in conjugal domesticity as was the norm and instead, carved out a role through religious austerities which gave her parity alongside the other male devotees of Sri Ramakrishna.

Lakshmimani Devi was born to Sri Ramakrishna's elder brother, Ramehswar, in Kamarpukur in 1864.[29] She had two older brothers, Ramlal and Shivaram. As a little girl, she would assist in the family duties of worshipping the family deities by picking flowers and making sandal paste. Her childhood was spent in solitude and in worship. These were acts of learning; she emulated what was the social norm around her and imbibed the spirit of devotion and worship. This would have been the usual lifestyle of young, girls from brahmanical families who lived in rural Bengal in the nineteenth century. She started school by learning to read the first primary book and she would share this knowledge with her aunt, Sri Sarada Devi, who was ten years older. Gender roles were quite distinct and girls were primarily seen as being involved in domestic labour. It comes as a surprise to learn that Sri Ramakrishna ensured that their education was continued when they went to Dakshineshwar, by hiring a young boy, Sharat Bhandari, who was their teacher. Most women would have been quite literate but by ensuring that they were taught by a

---

[29] For more on Lakshmi Devi, see Krishna Chandra Sengupta'a *Sri Sri Lakshmimani Devi* (Cuttack, 1943).

teacher, Sri Ramakrishna wanted them to have some kind of formal instructions.

During the monsoons, Sri Ramakrishna would leave Dakshineshwar for Kamarpukur. An event took place which altered Sri Ramakrishna's view on the conditions of the lives of women in his reasonably impoverished household. A particular kind of rice was served to their household deity Raghuvir, and the rice was over in the house. So, Ramehswar's wife asked Lakshmi to go over to the next village, Mukundapur, to buy some rice, which she did. But she was a thin, little girl of ten years old and her body was covered with a small cloth. Despite the fact that it was raining, the little girl left for the neighbouring village, carrying a bamboo basket on her head. She returned a bit later, without any rice and on seeing Sri Ramakrishna at the gate, burst into tears as she was unable to buy any rice. Sri Ramakrishna was extremely touched at this state of poverty and ensured that some property was bought so that the family deity could be served without any impediments. The women of the household were required to serve food, disregarding all the obstacles that they faced and Sri Ramakrishna's concern was a result of his comprehension that they had a very hard task doing so.

His acute awareness of what took place in the realm of the domestic and how it affected women helped him in comprehending how gender roles were prescribed by societal norms. Despite the fact that he spent his time in religious discourse and devotion, he did not separate himself from the everyday mundane. He closely interacted with village women and learnt about their lives and also gave them an opportunity to realise that there was more beyond the immediate. At Kamarpukur, he would spent time interacting with the village women, and in the process, learnt about their lives. He did not separate the spiritual/religious from the everyday, and in the act of engaging with the layperson, he undid his privilege as a religious teacher. The following incidents make that evident:

When Thakur was in his village, every evening he was in the habit of sitting by the door of his mother's home, watching the people as they passed along the street outside. All the women had to go that way to bring water from the tank. They would come with their jugs and seeing him at the door, they would sit down in the little yard in front with their water jugs beside them and forget everything in the joy of hearing him talk or sing of God. Fearing lest they might be neglecting their duties he asked concerning them. One girl said: "I have a cow. When I heard that you were coming I cut straw enough to last a month and filled my room with it." To another he said, " How is your baby?" "Oh! I forgot," she exclaimed. "I left it with a neighbour." She had walked more than a mile to come.

One day, Thakur said, "Now, today you must sing and I will listen." They all remained silent. Not one dared utter a sound. But there was one girl whom Thakur loved very much, so much that whenever she did not come, he would send for her. As soon as she saw that no one else would sing, she sang a song in a weak, high pitched, quavering voice. All the girls began to laugh at her, but when she had finished, Thakur was delighted. "See how great is her devotion," he exclaimed. "Just because I asked her she has sung so frankly and simply. She alone among you has true devotion."[30]

Sri Ramakrishna was aware of the fact that societal norms prescribed the behaviour of married women in rural Bengal; they were intimately involved in the economy of the house. In his conversations with these village women, what comes across is his concern for them and his advice that they listen to him only after they had finished their work. Through this act, he acknowledged the fact that domestic labour was as important as his own labour – of imparting spiritual knowledge.

---

[30] Ibid., pp. 230-231.

It therefore is not a surprise that Lakshmi Devi was tangentially involved in married domesticity; in fact she spent most of her life in her natal home. When Lakshmi Devi was married to Dhanakrishna Ghatak at the age of eleven, Sri Ramakrishna predicted that she would become a widow. After marriage, she stayed at Kamarpukur, and did not go to her husband's house at Goghat village. A few months after marriage, Dhanakrishna left the village in search of work and visited Lakshmi Devi at Kamarpukur; but he never returned. Subsequently, she was also forbidden by Sri Ramakrishna to inherit any part of her husband's property and she gave it all away to his family. Thus, Lakshmi Devi not only became a widow by the time she was twelve years of age, but also had no connection with her husband's family; she lived in her natal home all her life. But, her life was not one of oppression and subjugation, and in fact, a different picture emerges, as she was gradually drawn into a spiritual-religious life at Dakshineshwar.

The norm for young widowed, upper caste girls who lived in the nineteenth century would have been to live a life of austerities and penance, but Lakshmi Devi's life is unusual as she was supported by her extended family. After becoming a widow, she lived in Kamarpukur for three years, after which she moved over to Dakshineshwar to live with Sarada Devi. Her move to Calcutta meant that she was leaving behind her immediate family in rural Bengal and entering a world that was defined by Sri Ramakrishna. This world was made out of strangers who were all, in some way, devotees of Sri Ramakrishna. For a young girl, this must have been quite a liberating space, away from the social constraints that would have still be present in rural Bengal. That she was associated within the religious domain that was established by Sri Ramakrishna, made her immune from the societal norms that were prevalent in the nineteenth century.

As she was a lovely young girl, Sri Ramakrishna cautioned her to be careful and to be never alone while visiting religious places. She assisted Sarada Devi in looking after Sri Ramakrishna. They lived in the *nahabat*, a small house in the garden, and this also served not only as their bedroom, sometimes accommodating many female devotees, but also as a kitchen where groceries were stored and food cooked for Sri Ramakrishna. Lakshmi Devi was thus, involved in the domain of domesticity but in a different context altogether.

In this newly established realm of domesticity, Sri Ramakrishna was their teacher, thus revealing a heightened sense of empathy for them. He was also undoing his own gender privilege as a man. He insisted on ensuring that they woke up early from bed. He himself slept very little and even while it was dark, he would walk around the garden and call out to them to wake up. In winter, while they would pretend to be asleep, he would pour water under the door which would seep through the floor and wet their floor beds. Sri Ramakrishna taught them how to live in this newly established realm of the domestic which was made out of his disciples and devotees.

In the absence of the larger social structure that would have been present in their village in Kamarpukur, if Lakshmi Devi had been staying there, the multicultural social space of Calcutta became her village. Sri Ramakrishna was intimately connected with her overall education. While there would be *kirtan* in his room, he made sure that they also could hear the music from the *nahabat*; "if the women do not see or hear, how will they learn?"[31] He was aware of the need for exposing women to the larger world outside; and by doing so, ensured that they were not limited by what was the usual social norm for upper caste women of the nineteenth century.

Lakshmi Devi's education was such that she was well versed in Hindu religion. Sri Ramakrishna would teach them stories from the Ramayana and the Mahabharata and then would question them to ensure that they had learnt the stories. Sri Ramakrishna initiated her; on asking her as to which deity she loved the most, she replied,

---

[31] Swami Chetananda, p. 65.

Radha-Krishna, and she was given a mantra on that. Previously, she had received a Shakti mantra from a monk called Swami Purnananda.

She was also made to practise what were rituals of monks; while at Cossipore, where Sri Ramakrishna was staying while being treated for cancer, he told her to go begging from door to door, spreading God's name. She was also told only to visit the houses of the poor and not the rich and Lakshmi Devi did so. This act of a young woman, going out to strangers and begging, made her participate in the public. It was quite unimaginable for a young, upper caste widow to be out in the public in the nineteenth century, without being labelled as a prostitute, and Lakshmi Devi did so.

After Sri Ramakrishna passed away in 1886, she travelled around India with Sarada Devi and mostly stayed at Kamarpukur. By then, a new world had opened up with Swami Vivekananda and his journeys to the west, and Lakshmi Devi was also involved in that; Sister Nivedita described her in the following manner:

Sister Lucky, or Lakshmididi, as is the Indian form of her name, was indeed a niece of his [Sri Ramakrishna] and is still comparatively a young woman. She is widely sought after as a religious teacher and director, and is a most gifted and delightful companion. Sometimes, she will repeat page after page of some sacred dialogue, out of one of the *jatras,* or religious operas, or again she will make the quiet room ring with gentle merriment, as she poses the different members of the party in groups for religious tableaux. Now it is Kali, and again Saraswati; another time it will be Jagatddhatri, or yet again, Krishna under his *kadamba* tree, that she will arrange, with picturesque effect and scant dramatic material.[32]

---

[32] *The Complete Works of Sister Nivedita* (Sister Nivedita Girls School: Calcutta, 1967). p. 108.

We thus, learn, that she was a brilliant actress and storyteller, and these skills were used by her to disseminate religion. Within the intimate domain that was established by the devotees of Sri Ramakrishna, Lakshmi Devi was able to live a life that was far from the norm for young, brahmin widows of the nineteenth century in Bengal. Eventually, she moved to Puri in 1924 and lived the last years of her life there. She passed away in 1926.

5 YOGIN MA (1851-1924)

If you were born as a daughter in an upper middle class family in Calcutta in the middle of the nineteenth century, what options did you have? This is not a rhetorical question and the life of Yogindra Mohini Biswas, or Yogin-Ma as she was known, delineates a trajectory that was not the norm and outside the realm of blissful domesticity.[33] Yogindra Mohini Mittra was the daughter of Prasanna Kumar Mittra, a well known physician, working in Calcutta Medical College, with a specialization in midwifery. Calcutta Medical College was essentially a very British educational institution; during the years, 1844-45, there were nine teachers, most of whom were Britishers; there were two other Indians in the staff. One was Babu Dayal Chand Basak and the other was Prasanna Kumar Mitra, the resident surgeon of one of the hospitals. He was David Hare's favourite student, and attended to him while he was dying of cholera in 1842. Prasanna Mitra belonged to the Young Bengal movement, and was part of the circle called Derozians, who were quite vocal in espousing for social changes in all spheres of Bengali life, except in the realm of religion and gender (which is why Prasanna Mitra barely gave his daughter much of a formal education.) He was a member of the group that formed the Society of the Acquisition of General Knowledge in 1838 and by 1843, it had 200 members; Prasanna Mitra was one of the contributors.

---

[33] For more, see Swami Chetananda'a *They Lived with God: Life Stories of Some Devotees of Sri Ramakrishna* (Calcutta: Advaita Ashram, 1996), pp. 139-154.

Yogin-Ma was born on January 16, 1851 and her mother was the second wife of Prassana Mittra who was quite a wealthy man, and lived in Baghbazar, and was a neighbour of Balaram Basu, one of Sri Ramakrishna's household disciple. The division between the public world, where western education was the dominant norm, and the private realm, would have been enormous and despite the fact that her father was very educated, and part of the bag and baggage of western institutions like the Calcutta Medical College and the Young Bengal movement, Yogin-Ma did not really receive much of a formal education. So what exactly were her options and was she in any position to be an agent? Was she relegated absolutely and completely in the realm of the domestic and the private?

Yogin-Ma was married at the age of seven to Ambika Charan Biswas, an adopted son of a rich and well known family who lived in Khardah, a short distance away from Calcutta. Her husband's family was known for its philanthropy and piety and was well versed in Tantric philosophy. Yogin-Ma went to live with her husband when she had grown up, only to realise that her husband was a drunkard and a wastrel, quite profligate in his lifestyle. He squandered his inheritance quickly and was soon reduced to a pauper. His lifestyle was quite extravagant; he once asked a servant to light his hookah with five hundred bills. Ambika Charan seems to have participated in what was the normal *babu* behaviour. Yogin-Ma tried to initiate a change in his life but it really did not work out. She had a son, who died at the age of six months, and a daughter. She returned to her parental home and was welcomed by her mother.

We learn that the choices she could make were limited; her life would have been limited to bringing up children and raising them, as had been her mother's life. The fact that her personal life was quite broken did nudge her into making a spiritual shift. Gradually, she came to know about Sri Ramakrishna and Sri Sarada Devi. Her maternal grandmother was also familiar with this young priest from Dakshineshwar, mostly thought the newspaper writings of Keshab

Sen. This does say much about the fact that women were literate in the nineteenth century, even if they did not have much of any formal education; her grandmother would have lived in the early 1800s. She read journals and newspapers and learnt about Sri Ramakrishna through these printed texts. Therefore, Yogin-Ma might not have received much of any formal instructions but it would have been likely that she was educated at home.

Balaram Basu was her husband's maternal uncle, and also their neighbour in Baghbazar. Whenever Balarama Basu visited Sri Ramakrishna, she would also join the company along with other women. In her memoirs, she wrote:

> Gradually I began to feel an attraction for the Master. Just the thought of visiting him would make my mind dance with joy. On the day that I planned to go there I would get up early and finish my household duties as quickly as possible. My longing to see him knew no bounds. After arriving at his room I would forget everything, sitting in his presence. The master used to experience Samadhi off and on, and at that time we would look at his face with wonder. He was so compassionate! Whenever I brought him some ordinary preparations he would relish them like a young boy, saying joyfully, "Very tasty! Delicious!" And always at the time of our departure he would say, "Come back again."

> When I returned home after my first visit with the Master, I would spend the whole week in an intoxicated mood. This established a strong relationship. I cannot express the joy I felt. Even while I was engaged in cooking or other household activities, my mind was with the Master. After

some days, when I would feel my intoxication diminishing, my mind would again long to see him.[34]

This personal account reveals that Yogin-Ma's life was primarily defined by the fact that she was involved in the economy of the household and it was only after she finished her household chores that she could devote time to visit Sri Ramakrishna. She describes him as being "compassionate"; Sri Ramakrishna could identify with her and engage with her on her terms.

Gradually, Sri Ramakrishna started teaching her and revealed a world that was outside the realm of the domestic and the home. He taught her that if she meditated on him, it would be the equivalent of worshipping the *Devi mantram* that she had been taught by her husband's family's guru. He also showed her how to practise *japam*. Sri Ramakrishna suggested that she read the religious texts and she did labour towards reading the Ramayana and the Mahabharata, the Puranas, the Bhagavad Gita and so on.

She was also able to initiate some change in her husband, Ambika Charan Biswas, but eventually, he died due to fever; Yogin-Ma was involved in looking after him during this last phase of his life. Sri Ramakrishna was pleased with her acts of kindness and duty and visited her home on July 28th, 1885. Swami Akhandananda described an incident which reveals that not all in her family looked at Sri Ramakrishna with favour.

Once Sri Ramakarishna went to Yogin-Ma's house at Nebubagan, Baghbazar. Hiralal, a brother of Yogin-Ma's, did not like the fact that she went to Dakshineshwar. We heard that when Yogin-Ma invited the Master to her house, Hiralal brought a famous gymnast and wrestler named Manmatha,

---

[34] Quoted in Ibid., pp. 142, from Swami Nirlepananda's *Ramakrishna Bhaktamalika. Volume 2* (Karuna Prakashani: Calcutta, 1968), p. 15-16.

who lived in Gosaipara, to frighten him. After Manmatha saw the Master and heard a few words from him, he fell at his feet and said to him, weeping, "My Lord, I am guilty, Please forgive me." The Master replied, "All right. Come one day to Dakshineshwar."[35]

It is surprising that despite the fact that Yogin-Ma's family was quite intimate with Sri Ramakrishna, his brother disapproved of her visits to Dakshineshwar. Was it because she was seen as capable of receiving a spiritual education and thus, was an agent of her own? Or was it because she had acted independently and Hiralal did not approve of such independence? Or was it that Hiralal simply did not like Sri Ramakrishna? If not, then why was it so? It is not surprising to read incidents from Yogin-Ma's life where Sri Ramakrishna encouraged her to undo the societally accepted notions of gender normativity. Once, she along with some other women, visited Dakshineshwar where Sri Ramakrishna insisted that they visit the market and shop for vegetables which would be cooked for lunch; they did so despite the fact that they never went out without some form of purdah. It was almost as if Sri Ramakrishna himself could not fathom the societal need for purdah.

Yogin-Ma's description on how Sri Ramakrishna engaged with them is quite remarkable:

> Sometimes when I was with him I would feel that he was not a man but one of us [women]. Although it is natural for us to feel a certain shyness before men, we had no such feeling in the Master's presence. If perchance that feeling would arise, it would disappear immediately, and we would be free to open

---

[35] Quoted in Swami Chetanananda, p. 145, from Swami Akhandananda's *Smriti Katha* (Udbodhan: Calcutta, 1937), pp. 42-43.

our hearts to him. We used to speak to him about every intimate things, without any scruple or hesitation. And how kind, how affectionate, the Master was to us! When strangers, casually reading the life of Sri Ramakrishna, jump to the conclusion that he did not like women, we simply laugh.[36]

As she was unable to meditate and be involved in her *japam* in peace in Calcutta, she decided to go to Varanasi. After Sri Ramakrishna passed away in 1886, Sarada Devi joined her at Varanasi. It was here that the Holy Mother was told by Sri Ramakrishna, in a vision, to initiate Swami Yogananda and she did so, with Yogin-Ma's assistance. She was seen as an equal to Sri Ramakrishna.

The young monastic disciples looked upon Yogin-Ma as their own mother and would make demands on her. As she was a very good cook, everyone including Sarada Devi, loved her cooking. Swami Vivekananda would also make such childish requests to be fed well; once on his birthday he wanted her to make a rice pudding for him. The skills she learnt to be a cook were from within the realm of the domestic and she was able to reach out and feed a family that was outside the bonds of blood; even though she conformed to gender roles, she was able to subvert it by reaching out to a large group of people and receive appreciation.

Yogin-Ma was extremely perceptive and could see beyond the immediate obvious; once, her foot touched Swami Saradananda's cloth, and she immediately saluted him but he was hesitant to accept this. Yogin-Ma replied, "You are a monk. Your ochre robe is a symbol of renunciation. It is this renunciation that made Sri Ramakrishna great, and you are following in his footsteps. A little

---

[36] Quoted in Swami Chetananda, p. 147 in *Vedanta and the West. Volume 110* (Vedanta Press: Hollywood), p. 59.

cobra is as poisonous as a big cobra."[37] Despite being a householder in many respects and living a life that was constrained due to the fact that she was a woman, Yogin-Ma understood the fact that a monk, by the very act of renunciation, was superior to all.

Yogin-Ma was a householder in all overt respects, but she was quite nun-like in her behaviour. Even if institutionally, women in the nineteenth century did not have parity in the public realm, she was able to attain equality in the sphere of the spiritual, and alongside Swami Saradananda, on November 20th 1900, was initiated into *purna-abhisheka*, a Tantric rite, by Ishwar Chandra Chakravarty. Subsequently, in Puri, she was initiated into Vedic sannyasa by Swami Saradananda in the presence of Swami Premananda. Was there any need for these young monks to involve her in the rituals that were specific to their spiritual aspirations? The fact that they found it acceptable for a woman to be an equal in this realm speaks volumes on how Sri Ramakrishna influenced them.

Towards the end of her life, she was involved with a larger group of disciples, some of whom had come from the West. Sister Devamata described her in the following manner:

> Yogin-Ma always seemed to me one of the noblest of Sri Ramakrishna's disciples … She did not abandon her householder life, but no nun in a cloister was more rigid in her spiritual observance than she … Her householder life was lived with her aging mother in a modest home within walking distance of Holy Mother's quarters. She was punctiliously faithful in fulfilling her duty to her mother. No service was ever omitted, no care neglected. Her loving thought was constantly on her. But with more lingering persistence did it rest in the memory of her blessed association with Sri Ramakrishna. Since her first contact with him, her supreme interest had been

---

[37] Swami Chetananda, p. 150.

centred in her spiritual life. This, as I saw it, was lived at the Udbodhan Office in Mukherjee Lane, where, on the second story, Holy Mother was housed. These two parallel lines of living never crossed or clashed. Each seemed to strengthen and sweeten the other.

Her day was too well organized to permit of conflict. She rose before night had lifted and at four went for her bath in the Ganga. She never failed. Sometimes when she was not well, Swami Saradananda would remonstrate with her and beg her to consider her health; but she remained firm. The early bath in the Ganga, with its prayer and sacred chanting, was a religious duty and should not be put aside. The bath over, she returned to her home, gave her mother the necessary care, and at seven o clock she was climbing the stairs at the Udbodhan Office to carry a morning greeting to the Holy Mother. This done, she went below to a room underneath the stairs. Here she decided on the purchases to be made at the bazar and cut the vegetables for the noon meal. She regarded this as her special privilege. At about eleven she returned to the upper room to conduct the puja. ... The hour of prayer in that upper chamber where the shrine was, counted among the most precious in the day for me. Yogin-Ma and I were alone – she before the altar, I beside an inner window opening on the court. Holy Mother came and went. Others entered the room. It was all essentially informal, but Yogin-Ma's thought remained fixed on the puja. She was very strict in conforming with all the usages and traditions of worship. She would never speak while she was worshipping, and it seemed at times as if Holy Mother was teasing or testing her, for she would go up to her and ask her a question. Yogin-Ma would give a monosyllabic answer behind closed teeth without moving her lips. Mother would smile and walk away ...

After the puja Yogin-Ma served the noon meal – to the ladies in the front rooms near the shrine, to Swami Saradananda and the Udbodhan staff in a large dining room at the rear end of the story. When the meal was eaten, she went to her mother, but in the late afternoon she was back once more in the room under the stairs conferring with Swami Saradananda. This was the one hour of real recreation in all the day; for when they had disposed of immediate questions, they lived over again and yet again the blessed days with Sri Ramakrishna. They told each other stories of the Master they had heard a hundred times; they talked of Swamiji (Swami Vivekananda) and the other disciples who had gone; they spoke tenderly and devoutly of Holy Mother. It was a cherished hour – that hour spent together in the little room underneath the stairs. Arati (vesper service) seemed but the culmination of it, and Yogin-Ma passed half in dream from the memory of the Master to his worship in the shrine. With her heart aglow, she waved the incense and burning camphor before the picture; then with the same warmth of love she turned, when arati was over, to distribute the offered food to his children …[38]

If she had not met Sri Ramakrishna, her life would have been limited to the realm of Baghbazar and her parental home, and her labour would have been limited to raising children and maintaining a household; her life would really not have been any different from that of her mother. She would have strictly confined to gender roles. And yet, her life took another turn when she entered the world of Sri Ramakrishna and the young monks who would spread his message to the world. She was connected to the wider world and was an agent in it; herself an equal and at par with the other monks and also involved in determining how worship would take place.

---

[38] Ibid., p. 150-152, from *Prabuddha Bharata*, 1932, pp. 456-58.

Her daughter, Ganu passed away in 1909, and with Swami Saradananda's help, she raised three grandsons. She went on pilgrimages all across India -- from Kedarnath in the north to Kanyakumari in the south. More importantly, she was quite involved in the intellectual ambience of the Udbodhan Office, where magazines were printed. When Swami Saradananda started work on *Sri Sri Ramakrishna Lilaprasanga* (*Sri Ramakrishna, The Great Master*), she was asked for her memories of the Master. She was therefore, involved in documenting the life of Sri Ramakrishna. The book was published periodically in the Bengali magazine, *Udbodhan*, and Yogin-Ma would hear the manuscript before it hit the presses. She also helped Sister Nivedita when she wrote *Cradle Tales of Hinduism*; Yogin-Ma had a prodigious memory and remembered incidents form all the religious texts. All the events in the personal life, thus, reached out to a larger global readership through this realm of the intellect and printed texts.

She passed away on June 4th, 1924 at the Udbodhan house.

6 CONCLUSION

Was Sri Ramakrishna socially transgressive? Or did he conform to the status quo, and was he complicit with institutions of patriarchy? The Widow Remarriage Act was passed in 1856. Sri Ramakrishna's niece, Lakshmimani Devi, became a child widow at the age twelve in 1876, twenty years after the Bill was passed. Lakshmi Devi remained a widow her whole life; she never stayed at her in-laws house and had access to the public domain of religion that was established by Sri Ramakrishna in Dakshineshwar . She herself was intimately involved in the life of Sri Ramakrishna, assisting Sarada Devi in looking after his needs. Was she an agent, able to determine certain choices in her life? Undoubtedly, she was limited to the choices she could have made, being born to a very religious, brahmin family in rural Bengal, and becoming a widow when she was young. Under Sri Ramakrishna, she entered the world of Hinduism as he was redefining it, and was treated, on many ground, at par like his male disciples.

If we recuperate the life of Yogin-Ma's father, Prasanna Mitra, we learn about the socio-cultural conditions under which she was raised and the fact that she did not have access to the public realm which had been established by her father. Prasanna Mitra belonged to the generation of the Young Bengals and worked at the Calcutta Medical College; Yogin-Ma did not have access to these realms of the public because she was a woman.

How was it to be a woman in nineteenth century Bengal, India?

Retrieving the lives of two female disciples of Sri Ramakrishna

www.ingramcontent.com/pod-product-compliance
Lightning Source LLC
Chambersburg PA
CBHW071748020426
42331CB00008B/2224